Let's Reflect

On

Life!

Birister Sharma

Dedicated to my loving wife....

Pallabi Devi Sharma

I surrendered to you, O my Lord......

"Om Namah Shivaya"

Table of Contents

One Word

You've to awake yourself.

You've to arise yourself.

You've to know yourself.

You've to find out yourself.

You can't live your life without reflection on your life. Without the reflection on your life, you couldn't find meaning and direction. Without the reflection on your life, you couldn't unearth your inner strength and potential.

It is only the reflection on your life which makes you aware in your life. It is only the reflection on your life which makes your life purposeful, and shows you the right direction. With the reflection of life you can set your goals of life and move ahead in your life.

Your reflection on life makes you realize what you've to do with your life. You'll know what is right for you, and what is wrong for you.

---***---

1. Actions

Be always careful in your life.

Whatever you do in your life whether good or bad, everything reflects back to you.

If you do good things in your life, good things will always reflect back to you.

If you do bad things in your life, bad things will always reflect back to you.

Your life is like a mirror whatever you want to see in your life, you'll see yourself in the mirror of your life.

If you grow a fruit plant, you'll always get the delicious fruits.

If you grow a thorny bush, you'll always get the nail like thorns.

Your life is always on your hands.

If you play your life with the ball of fire, you'll always get burn.

If you play your life with the naked knife, you'll always get hurt.

But if you love your life, your life will always love you back. If you care your life, your life will always care you.

The way you will treat your life, the way your life will treat you back. Never try to do anything against your life.

---***---

Anecdote:

A father and his son are walking in a mountain area. Suddenly the son falls, hurts himself and screams: "AAAhhhhhhhhhh!!!"

To his surprise, he hears a voice repeating, somewhere in the mountain: ""AAAhhhhhhhhhh!!!" Curiously, he yells: "Who are you?"

He receives the answer: "Who are you?"

Angered at the response, he screams; "Coward!"

He receives an answer matching his: "Coward!"

He looks at his father and asks: "What's going on?"

The father, smiling, says: "My son, pay attention." And he cries to the mountain: "I admire you!" "I admire you!"

The father shouts: "You are a champion!"

The voice answers: "You are a champion!"

The boy is surprised, but doesn't understand.

Then the father explains: "People call this an echo, but really this is life. It gives you back everything you say or do."

---***---

Reflect on your life:

Be always careful in your life.

Whatever you do in your life whether good or bad, everything reflects back to you.

---***---

2. Inner strength

If you want to rise in your life, then it is only your inner strength which alleviates you to rise up.

Your inner strength is the source of your growth in your life.

Your inner strength is your energy.

Your inner strength is your power.

Your inner strength is your belief.

Your inner strength is your confidence.

Your inner strength is your enthusiasm.

If you want to succeed in your life, then attain your inner strength.

If you want to achieve something great in your life, then unearth your inner strength.

If you've inner strength, then no external force will ever dare to waggle you whatever happens in your life.

Your inner strength will always boost you up in every situation.

It is only your inner strength which embraces you mentally and physically.

Your inner strength is the only source of your existence.

---***---

Anecdote:

Once a little boy was watching the balloon man at the country fair. The man was evidently a good salesman, because he allowed a red balloon to get loose and sour high up in the air- thereby attracting a crowd of perspective young customers.

Next he released a blue balloon, then a yellow one and a white one. They all went souring up into the sky until they disappeared. The little boy stood looking at the black balloon for a long time, then asked, "Sir, if you sent the black balloon up, would it go as high as the others?"

The balloon man gave the kid an understanding smile. He snapped the string that held the black balloon in place, and as it soured upwards, said, "It's not the color, son. It's what's inside that makes it rise."

---***---

Reflect on your life:

If you want to succeed in your life, then attain your inner strength.

If you want to achieve something great in your life, then unearth your inner strength.

---***---

3. Encourage

Your life is always a mystery. You never know what will happen next.

Your life is always up and down.

Sometimes its graphs will rise; and sometimes its graphs will fall.

You never stop the pendulum of your life.

You never cease the tides of your life.

But one thing you can always do, that is to encourage yourself.

Encourage yourself no matter whatever happens in your life.

If you fail in every endeavor of your life, even never stop to encourage yourself.

Your encouragement is the ladder of your success.

Your encouragement is the strength of your weakness.

Your encouragement is your energy.

Your encouragement is your power.

Your encouragement is your enthusiasm.

If you ever fall down in the middle of the crossroad of your life, then nobody will pull you up,

It is only your encouragement which will hold you firmly.

Your encouragement is your courage.

Encourage yourself whatever happens in your life.

---***---

Anecdote:

A group of frogs were travelling through the woods, and two of them fell into a deep pit. When the other frogs saw how deep the pit was, they told the two frogs that they were as good as dead. The two frogs ignored the comments and tried with all their might to jump up out of the pit. The other frogs kept telling them to stop, that they were as good as dead.

Finally, one of the frogs took heed to what the other frogs were saying and gave up. He fell down and died. The other frog continued to jump as hard as he could. Again, the crowd of frogs' yelled at him to stop the pain and just die. But he jumped even harder and finally made it out.

When he got out, he explained to the others that he was deaf. He thought they were encouraging him the entire time.

---***---

Reflect on your life:

Encourage yourself no matter whatsoever happens in your life.

If you fail in every endeavor of your life, even never stop to encourage yourself.

Your encouragement is the ladder of your success.

---***---

4. Limit

Discover your hidden potentials

You've infinite energy and power within you.

You just need to unearth (discover) it from deep inside you.

You've to dig it out.

You never reach anywhere if you're not aware of your potentials.

You've to seek it both internally and externally.

If you try, you can figure it out.

Your potentials are the wings of your life, without it you'll never fly.

You'll never touch the sky of your success.

One day you'll die like the crawling ants and insects.

You've every right to do something great in your life.

You're born to make your life beautiful and meaningful.

But until you would not know your true potentials, you would not do anything in your life.

Your life will become directionless.

Your life will become worthless.

Make it purposeful.

It is only your potentials which will gear you up.

Try to discover your hidden potentials, and sour the wide blue sky.

---***---

Anecdote:

A man found an eagle egg and placed it under a brooding hen. The baby eagle hatched with the chickens and grew to be like them. It clucked and stretched the earth for worms; flapped its wings and managed to fly a few feet in the air. Years passed.

One day, the eagle, now grown older, saw magnificent bird above it in the sky. It glided in graceful majesty against the powerful wind, with scarcely a movement of its golden wings. Spellbound, the eagle asked, "Who is that?"

"That's the king of birds, the eagle." said its neighbor. "It belongs to the sky. We belong to earth- we are chickens."

So the eagle lived and died as a chicken, for that's what it thought it was. The eagle reared and nurtured among the chicken was unaware of its true potentials. So it never learned to fly. How sad and shocking!

---***---

Reflect on your life:

You've infinite energy and power within you.

You just need to unearth it from deep inside you.

---***---

5. Luck

Never seek for your luck.

Your luck will seek you itself if you deserve for it.

Never wait for your luck.

Your luck will wait for you if you're worthy of it.

Only a foolish man waits for his luck.

But a wise man never waits for his luck, because he creates his own luck.

Your luck is disguised in the form of your hard works.

Your luck is much closer to you if you know how to make it yourself.

Your luck will find you itself.

You just need to toil, and open your heart, mind and soul.

Keep your nerves cool and calm.

Sometimes your luck doesn't show her appearance so easily.

You've to keep your patience.

Nobody is lucky or unlucky. It always depends on one's hard works.

Your luck will not decide to come to you,

But your hard works will force your luck to come to you.

See the difference.

Luck will smile itself.

---***---

Anecdote:

One morning before sunrise, a fisherman arrived at a river bank. While walking along, he stumbled against something and saw a small sack of stones. He picked up the sack, and putting his net aside, sat down to wait for the sunrise in order to start his day's work. Idly he picked a stone from the bag and threw it into the quiet river. Then he cast another stone and then another. In the silence of the early morning he liked the splashing sound, so he kept tossing the stones into the water one by one.

Slowly the sun rose and became bright. By then he had thrown away all the stones except one; the last stone lay in his hand. He was breathless when he saw by the daylight what he held in his hand. It was a diamond. He had thrown away a whole sack of them and this was the last piece. His heart almost failed him. He shouted. He cried. He had accidently stumbled upon so much wealth that his life would have been enriched many times over. But in the darkness, unknowingly, he had thrown it all away.

---***---

Reflect on your life:

Your luck is disguised in the form of your hard works.

Your luck is much closer to you if you know how to make it yourself.

Your luck will find you itself.

---***---

6. Time

Time takes own pace. It never moves too fast or too slow.

It always follows its natural order, and maintains its continuity.

Whatever happens in your life is always happened in time, neither before time nor after time.

Have you ever seen any season arrive before its time? A season never arrives before its own time.

Take your time whatever you think or act in your life. Follow your own pace. Never try to race.

You grow with time. You learn with time. You mature with time.

Try to understand yourself and your time. And utilize it in your own way. Always try to become natural.

If you know how to use your time you'll learn how to live your life.

You will take good decisions when you take your own time. And you will take wrong decisions when you do not take your own time.

You'll grow in your life when you take your own time. You'll mature in your life when you take your own time. A fruit never ripen before time. It takes own time.

You too take your own time; never try to run too fast that you'll miss your own natural talents and abilities.

---***---

Anecdote:

Once there lived a great king in the Himalayan Mountains. He wanted to select a man from his subjects to be his prime minister. When the search finally narrowed down to just three men, he decided to put them to a test. Accordingly, he placed them together in a room in his palace, and on the room door he installed a lock which was the last word in mechanical ingenuity.

The candidates were informed that whoever was able to open the door first would be appointed to the post of prime minister. The three men immediately set themselves to the task. Two of them began at once to work out a complicated mathematical formula to discover the proper lock combination. The third man, however, just sat in his chair, lost in thought. Then he walked to the door and turned the handle. And the door opened to his touch. It had been unlocked all the time.

---***---

Reflect on your life:

Try to understand yourself and your time. And utilize it in your own way.

If you know how to use your time you'll learn how to live your life.

Always try to become natural.

---***---

7. Don't rush

Look at the sun, the moon, the plants, and the trees, how they grow slowly and silently.

Do you ever see them growing in a hurry?

They never get in a hurry. They take their own time and pace.

In the same way you should try to grow slowly and silently while taking your own time, but try to grow continuously.

The river is always flowing slowly and silently. It never flows away fast or gets in a hurry. But it reaches to its destiny at the end, and confluences with the mighty ocean.

You never grow in a day or overnight. You never accomplish your work in a day or overnight.

You never get success in a day or overnight. You never reach anywhere in a day or overnight.

You'll burn your own fingers if you try to taste a hot dish in a hurry.

You've to take your own time. You never get anything in a hurry.

Even you're not grown up in a day or overnight.

Learn to grow slowly and silently. Never get in a hurry for anything.

Hurry brings you nothing but worry.

---***---

Anecdote:

A man who was very fond of trees wanted to see a green tree in the courtyard of his home. He thought that if he planted a sapling, it would take a long time to grow into a tree. So he went to a garden and selected a fully grown tree. He then employed several laborers to dig it up and then transport it to his courtyard where he had it planted. The man was very happy.

He thought to himself: "I have travelled a long journey in a single day. Planting a sapling or seed would have been a lengthy business but now I have found a quick way to have a lush green tree."

But, the next morning, when he looked at the tree, he found that its leaves had begun to wither, and after a few days the whole tree dried up. He was disappointed.

One of his friends visited him and found him in a very sad mood. When he asked the man the reason, he said, "I was in a hurry, but God isn't"

---***---

Reflect on your life:

You've to take your own time. You never get anything in a hurry.

Even you're not grown up in a day or overnight.

Hurry brings you nothing but worry.

---***---

8. Change

Change is the universal law.

You've to change with time.

You've to change with the situation.

You've to change with your requirements.

Always try to change yourself for good reasons. But never try to change yourself for wrong reasons.

It will always bring you unhappiness and discontentment.

Always try to change yourself. But never try to change anybody.

You can change yourself. But you never change anybody.

Change yourself internally. But never change yourself externally.

Change your mindsets for good. Change your perspectives for good.

Change your thoughts for good.

Change your ideas for good. Change your plans for good.

Change your decisions for good. Change your works for good.

Change your deeds for good.

But never get afraid to change yourself for good, because only your good change will bring a huge difference in this world.

---***---

Anecdote:

There was once a king who ruled a prosperous kingdom. One day he went on a trip to the distant areas of his kingdom. When he got back, he complained that his feet were badly bruised because it was the first time he had gone on such a long trip, and the road that he travelled was rough and stony. He then ordered his people to cover every road of the entire country with leather. This would need thousands of animal skins and would cost a huge amount of money.

One wise servant dared to suggest to the king, "Why do you have to spend such an unnecessary amount of money? Why don't we just cut a little piece of leather to cover your feet?"

The king was surprised, but agreed to his suggestion to make "shoes" for himself.

---***---

Reflect on your life:

You've to change with time.

Always try to change yourself for good reasons.

But never try to change yourself for wrong reasons.

Never get afraid to change yourself for good, because only your good change will bring a huge difference in this world.

---***---

9. Bad Habits

Your habits are very powerful. The way you cultivate your habits the way you become. Always nurture good habits in your life.

Your good habits will always lead you to the door of your happiness and success. But your bad habits will always lead you to the door of your unhappiness and failure.

Your good habits will enrich your entire life. But your bad habits will spoil your entire life.

Your good habits are like your best friends. But your bad habits are like your worse foes.

If you cultivate good habits in your life, you'll ever meet with good fortunes. On the other hand, if you cultivate bad habits in your life, you'll ever meet with bad fortunes.

Never allow any bad habit to dwell in you, because once it starts dwelling inside you, it'll eat you up completely like a beetle eat up a big tree.

Your bad habits will make your life hollow and worthless.

Good habits make good life. And bad habits make bad life.

Never allow your habits to control you, but control your own habits. Never become a slave of your habits, but ever become a master of your habits.

Only your good habits make your life beautiful and meaningful.

---***---

Anecdote:

A little banyan seed said to a palm tree one day, "I am tired of being tossed about by the wind; let me lodge in your branches."

"Stay as long as you like; be my guest," was the reply. Soon the tree forgot all about its tiny guest, but the seed did not remain idle. Immediately, it began to work its roots under the bark and into the heart of the trunk itself.

Finally the palm tree cried out, "What are you doing?"

"I'm only the little seed you allowed to rest among your branches," came the reply.

"I cannot leave you now," said the banyan. "We have grown up together, and it would kill you if I tore myself away now."

The tree tried desperately to shake itself loose, but to no avail. Eventually its graceful leaves turned brown and its trunk wasted away; but the banyan continued to thrive until its host could no longer be seen.

---***---

Reflect on your life:

Your habits are very powerful. The way you cultivate your habits the way you become.

Good habits make good life. And bad habits make bad life.

Never allow your habits to control you, but control your habits.

---***---

10. Hidden Talents

You're born with natural talents.

You've infinite potentials hidden within you.

You've hidden energy within you. You've hidden power within you.

You've to awake your sleeping natural talents.

You've to raise your laying natural talents.

You've to ignite your dormant natural talents.

You've to know the secrets of your natural talents.

You've to uncover your unseen natural talents.

You're born to do something great in this world.

If you do not awake your natural talents today, then you'll never explore the beauties and adventures of this world.

Your life will always engulf with darkness. You'll never see the happiness of your delights.

You'll never see the glorious arts of Almighty God in this world.

You'll never enjoy the marvelous creations of Almighty God in this world.

Awake your natural talents, and enjoy the beauties of this world.

---***---

Anecdote:

There was once a cave that lived underground, as most caves does. Since it had spent its entire life in darkness, it had never seen any light.

One day, a voice said to the cave, "Come up into the light. Come and enjoy the sunlight."

The cave replied, "I do not know what you mean by light. All I have ever known is darkness."

"Come and see for yourself," said the voice.

The cave mustered up enough courage to climb slowly up from the depths of the earth. Suddenly, it reached the top of the earth and was surrounded by magnificent light, which the cave had never seen in its life.

"This is beautiful," said the cave. After enjoying the light for a while, the cave said to the sunlight, "Now it's your turn to come with me and see the darkness."

"What is darkness?" asked the sunlight.

The cave answered, "Come and see it yourself."

So the sunlight decided to visit the cave's home. As the sunlight entered the cave, it said, "Now show me your darkness." But, with the sunlight, there was no darkness to be found!

---***---

Reflect on your life:

You're born with natural talents.

You've infinite potentials hidden within you.

You've to awake your sleeping natural talents.

Awake your natural talents, and enjoy the beauties of this world.

---***---

About the author:

Birister Sharma is a full time author. He is also an avid reader. He loves reading, writing, and motivation. He has penned down dozens of self-help motivational books and novels so far.

You may contact him @ birister2007@gmail.com